*Prayers from
a Searching Heart*

PRAYERS FROM
A SEARCHING HEART

Ian Calvert

Illustrated by Mary Romans

Darton Longman and Todd
London

First published in 1985 by
Darton Longman and Todd Ltd
89 Lillie Road, London SW6 1UD

© 1985 Ian Calvert

Illustrations © 1985 Mary Romans

ISBN 0 232 51659 6

British Library Cataloguing in Publication Data

Calvert, Ian
  Prayers from a searching heart.
  1. Devotional literature
  I. Title
  242   BV4832.2

  ISBN 0–232–51659–6

Photypeset by Input Typesetting Ltd, London
SW19 8DR
Printed and bound in Great Britain by
Anchor Brendon Ltd, Tiptree, Essex

Contents

Introduction

It used to be the claim of a leading Sunday news-paper that 'all human life is here'. Of course, it was not and never could be, just as it never could be in the pages of *Prayers from a Searching Heart*.

Yet this has been the aim in compiling the poems which make up this book. I have tried to contain within them as many varied experiences and thoughts as possible. They come from a heart that is sure that God is with us always, everywhere and at all times. But God's will, his purpose and actions may not always be clear and obvious. He calls us to seek, to follow and to find him. In this task *Prayers from a Searching Heart* tries to be a signpost pointing the ways to God. Its arms are the poems to warm our hearts and give direction to our prayers. I want you to read one of the poems, as you feel led, or as you have need. Having read it, ponder upon the message that comes to you through it and, in pondering, pray. Remember Mother Mary Clare's first lesson in prayer: 'that it is God's activity in us, and not a self-activated process of our own'. The poems can help us to lay ourselves open to God.

In this way my book can be everyone's book, for we are all of us seekers. We are all of us on a journey to God, each on our own journey, each journey at our own pace; and on the journey each of us will have individual experiences, joys, sorrows, successes and failures, and each our own needs. It is my hope that these prayer-poems will help your prayers as you make your journey and clarify your vision of God's purpose for his world and for you.

I too am making the journey. I am heartened to know that through this book we are making the journey together; and I am grateful for the opportunity of exploration which writing the book has given me.

Ian Calvert
Easter 1985

Now is the day of our farewell in fear,
lean pages; and shall I leave some
blessing on the half of me you have
devoured?

Thomas Merton, 'The Poet to his book'

God and me

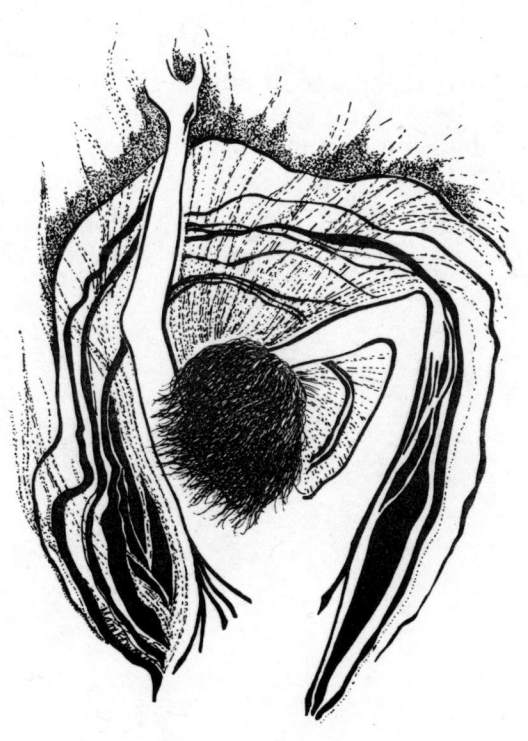

'Good God!'

Why do you say
'Good God!'
When you're surprised
Or hurt
By something you cannot understand?
If there were no God,
Or if God were not good,
Why, then there'd be
No problem.

'Yes' to God

I met someone.

He said 'Come with me',
When I was going
The other way.

He said 'Do this for me',
When I was doing something else.

He said 'Say this in my name',
When I wanted to say
Just the opposite.

He said 'Be this',
When I did not think
That I could.

But I went, did and was,
For I said
'Yes' to God.

A daylight atheist

I'm a daylight atheist
And fine.
In the warmth, the light and the sun
What need I of God
With my health and my strength?
They'll last me
Till day is done.

But when it grows dusk,
Sun sinks,
Shadows fall.
Then wonder and doubt
Of what life's all about
Starts clouding and crowding
My mind.

And when it grows night,
Clouds race o'er the moon
And light
Alternates with dark.
Then trees look giants,
Rocks cliffs,
Then life takes on
A new look.

Oh being an atheist
Is fine and grand
When sunshine bathes the land.
But it isn't much fun
When there's no longer sun,
Facing problems and ills
In the dark.

God of the dazzling darkness

God
You are too deep for me,
Too high for me,
Too bright, and yet too dark for me.

Should I plunge
I cannot see your shape.
Should I run
I cannot breathe your air.
Should I climb
I cannot attain you.

Your darkness overpowers,
Envelops, overlies me,
Yet forward alone is the way.
Blinded by your light,
I cannot see the source
From which it comes.

You who are the unknowable,
The indiscernible, the unimaginable,
Whom to describe, measure or fathom
Is to demean,
Reach out your hand
To steer me through the deeps,
So I may scramble to the heights,
Unseeing, unknowing, yet longing.
You, God of the deep
But dazzling darkness.

The silence of God

Being silent
Is one thing
Living with silence
Quite another.
The first I choose
The second is chosen for me.

I may choose
Whether I speak or no,
Am quiet or noisy
Chatter or am still.

But speak and wait
For an answer –
That, I cannot control.

All I can do is wait
Wait for the one I've addressed
To reply
Give some sign
That I've been heard
Heard and understood.

But when that One
Is God
And there's no reply
Just silence
Silence more silent than a wall
Which at the very least
Echoes your voice,
What then?

It's hard to live
With the silence of God
It's the greatest test of all
For it's hard to be sure
That the love of God
Can overleap
Has overleaped
That wall.

A tightrope of faith

I feel that I'm walking
A tightrope of faith,
Whether to believe or no.
The wire stretched ahead
Is all that I've got,
But it's an awful long way
To fall.

I can't see the end.
There's no going back
And if I stand still
I'll drop.
So there's only ahead
And forward
To answer your call.

But will you be there
When I get to the end
And make my journey worthwhile?
Is my vision true?
My vision of you
And my steps on the wire
Safe and sure?

Sometimes you're so clear
I could skip to the pole.
But then I look down
Fearing Peterlike
I'll drown.
Will I ever, I ask,
Make the end?

Could I only see
That you're always with me
And I don't have to wait
For my friend.

Time's endless stream

Time's endless stream

Time's stream surrounds us
Before, around and behind
A ceaseless, changing flow.
Now, flushed with overnight rain,
Turbulent, brown.
Now tranquilly, clear and slow.

Sometimes reflecting
A hastening cloud
Or revealing in depths below
The trout's tail flick
Darting upstream
Clearing the slow, steady flow.

So runs time
In our lives
Whether troubled, serene or secure
Over rock and through pool
On to the ocean sure.

Back we the stream
Of what might have been
Or face we
Whatever may come?
Be we chronicler or seer
Looking back or afore
God leaves us the choice
When day's done.

The dawn's a friend

Our milkman called
At half past four.
I heard the bottles
By the door.

He came that time
With boot steps quick.
I heard him then
For I was sick.

But now I'm well
He comes no more.
I miss his boot steps
At the door.

Oh, when you're ill
The dawn's a friend.
Another sleepless night
Is at an end.

And friends are those
Who bring it in.
Welcome those boots
And bottles' din.

Hello, day

Waking up
I say
'Hello, day'.
What will you bring
Today?

Will it be
Like a menu
Planned and timed
In my diary?

Will it be
Like yesterday
And every day before
Predictable, reliable
Or boring?

Or will it be
Quite new
Like a recipe
I've made up
For the very first time?

Whatever it may be
What matters
Is what I make of it
What I put into it
And how I value it.

Hello, day.
Thank you for coming.

Halftime is a good time

It's lunchtime
Halfway through the day.
I haven't half completed
All I planned
On the way.

Why am I
So unrealistic
How much on that way
I'll achieve?
And why so quickly diverted
From the end in which I believe?

Yes, halftime
Is a good time
For looking
Backwards and fore,
For becoming
Clear and pragmatic
As you rest before starting
Once more.

That's it

That's it.
Nothing more today.
What's not
Been accomplished now
Must wait
Another day.

That's it.
It could have been
Better done.
But there's my day, Lord,
Warts and all,
Another battle won.

But, then,
Come to think of it
It could have been
Much worse.
Just imagine
What might have been
Simply left to myself.

Be with me, Lord, for ever
For ever, till the morn
That morn
You come to tell me
That – that's it.

Good night.

'As long as this world lasts'

Some say
'Till the end of the world',
While others
'As long as this world lasts'.
There's a difference between them,
You know.

For the first
Is God's doing,
While the second
Is ours.
The first is planned,
While the second occurs.

For God's end will come
In his own good time
When all will be made anew.
But man's end will dawn
When we've raped the earth
Polluted the sea
And pressed the wrong button
Too soon.

Lord, give us the wisdom
And give us the grace
To have the patience
The strength and the love
So we're finally there
And that our world lasts
Until yours ends.

*Listen to
the city*

Listen to the city

Listen to the city
Anytown, Notown, Downtown
Mark its tinged cry.

The city's
Like an orchestra
Tuning up to play.
Some parts big and brassy
Others with hardly a say.
Some take melody's high road
Others are just by the way.

Oh listen to the tuba,
Piccolo and viol
One and all a soloist
Each to his own style.

But when the tuning's over
The orchestra plays as one.
Not so Downtown city
Where each is for his own,
Where practice notes are the real thing
And soloists play on.

Oh listen to the city
Mark its tinged cry.

Pray in the tension

Today
Many of us live
A nation of strangers,
Aliens in cities,
Trapped in societies
Of rapid, social change.

Constantly
We face new problems
With no clear answers.
It's not happened
To us before.
Nobody's behaved
Like that before.
We've got
No tailormade pattern.

It's an itsy bitsy life.
Let's be quite clear,
No comprehensive lifestyles
No grand, universal designs
Let's not look for them.

Rather
Let's get clear the tension
Between heaven and earth,
Between our visions
Of God and the earth,
And the tension
Of fidelity to both.
And in the tension
Pray.

The only one in town

I must be
The only one in town
That hasn't gone away
That's got no one
They can ring
On this Bank Holiday.

I thought the day
My man walked out
That all would be sublime
I never thought
I'd miss him so
In quite so short a time.

I thought, at last
I would be free
To go out with my friends
But when I came to fix it up
They'd all got other ends.

Di is in Gibraltar
While Jo is at her gran's
And Clare is in the country
She's got other plans.
And me, yes me,
Whatever am I at?
I don't need long to tell you,
Stuck here alone in this flat.

I'm sure
I should be grateful
I've everything
Just pat.
If only it wasn't so hateful
To be all by myself
With the cat.

Of course
Bank Holiday's soon over.
Anyway, it's going to rain.
Soon everyone is going to be back
And life
Will start up again.

But loneliness, the loneliness
Will it too go away?
Or shall I have it
Round my neck
For ever and a day?

I'll not give in
And ring him up
To give it another try.
But I've got to do something
Pretty sharp,
For I'm so very
Very very lonely.

Did that phone ring?
Don't be daft –
Of course it didn't!

In the city

In the city
I've learned
That the desert is
Just wherever you are.
For the desert I mean
Is not the absence of men
But rather
The presence of God.

But, how do you see
This desert of God
How can you know
That it's there?
Just look for the solitude
Within your heart.

Seek a calm, tranquil stillness.
In terrace-row home,
On Wimpey estate
Or fifteenth-floor flat,
You don't look for God.
He's waiting for you
Just as soon
As you come through the door.

Be still
And know.

To a messenger

Just say
You saw me.
You spoke to me.
You know I'm here.

Don't come back
And tell me
You forgot.

I matter.
I'm a person
Though I may not be much.
Just a bundle of rags,
Held together by string.

I sleep
Under the railway arch
In a cardboard box.
And I live
On cidar and gin.

It's no sort of life,
I know.
But it's that
To which I've grown used.
I don't feel the cold any more.

I can't last much longer.
I can feel that
In my bones.
But that's why it's important

That someone knows
I'm here.
Because I'm a person,
And I matter.

I've become used to it

Each day
I see
As I go on my way
Legacies
Of today's way of living.

And, what bothers me most
I just pass by
I've become used to it
I just don't care
Any more.

I've become used
To teenagers
With nothing to do
Propping up street corners,
Mugging for drugs
Soliciting for pimps and thugs.

I've become used
To young mothers
In underground subways
Babes akimbo
Hands clutching for cash.

I've become used
To winos slumped on steps,
Whining for change
Through cider-moistened lips
Or sleeping the morning away.

O why don't I care
Any more
What another's fate is,
Hardly glancing
As I pass by?

And why can't I see
In another's agony
Reflections
Of my agony too?

You don't like your job

You don't like your job
In the city.
You hate the underground ride,
You dislike what you call
The rat race.
But then,
You've got your pride.

Alternatives
Might not be easy,
So you hang on
To what you've got.
But do your feelings
Take over
How you do it?
You don't care
If it all goes to pot.

But you've decided
There's no way round it,
You've decided
To say where you are.
So why sulk
Through what is
Inevitable?
That won't shorten it
By even one hour.

Pray you well for your city

The city's a sieve,
So I read in a book,
And a magnifier too.
The dross of the world
Gets caught in its mesh.
The ore of the gospel
Gets through.

That precious
Ore of the gospel
Separated by city sieve
Inspires the city's existence
Enabling man to live.

A magnifier too
Is the city
Making life's particles clear.
You can see what they're like
And of what they are made,
The gospel's share of the year.

Some sieves
That I know
Are rustbound
Broken and holed
And quite unable to sieve.
Ore and dross become merged
Spreading dust unrefined and
Choke man's capacity to live.

But whatever the state
Of the ore or the dust
No matter how rusty the sieve,
The city continues, enlarging
The conditions in which
Men live.

Oh pray you well
For your city
And the folk
Who people its ways,
That God's message
Continually guide it,
Bringing justice and peace
In our days.

Be at peace, bring peace

Do you feel in the city
That you're wasting your time
If you're not doing something?
Do you get anxious, frustrated, tense
And start to perform
Just to justify yourself?

Can't you see,
Oh can't you see?
All you need
Is to be.

Just be yourself to people,
For the presence of one
In love with God,
Walking with folk,
Is God's plenty indeed.

So be at peace,
Bring peace,
Even with nothing to do.

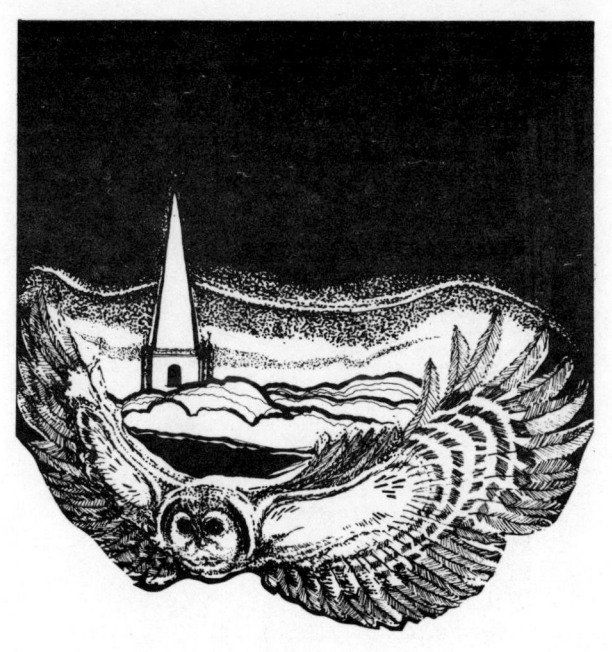

Listen to the silence

Listen to the silence

Listen to the silence
Of land at evening time.
Listen as the fading light
Silhouettes the sentinel pine.

Listen to the silence
As bats fly to and fro
And hunting owls glide noiselessly
Surveying fields below.

Listen to the silence
As hunting, hunted seek
Their prey, their rest,
The strong to trap the weak.

Listen to the silence.
The village falls asleep
And church-bell's chime
Rings out the day
As lovers homeward creep.

Listen to the silence
As dawn gives place to day,
And grazing cattle start to crop,
A donkey starts to bray.

Listen to the silence
It's far, around and near.
A world of stillness night and day
If only we will hear.

Ebb and flow

Ebb and flow,
Ebb and flow,
Like the tide
Like time
Like eternity
Like the saints, their lands, their homes.
Earthbound I
With the tips of my fingers
Can touch their world,
Can raise myself
Briefly to glimpse over the edge
Fall back and sink content
Knowing it's there.
Ebb and flow, ebb and flow.

I passed a tree

I passed a tree this afternoon
Raised by the soil,
The sun and the rain.
Aslant to the ground
Shaped by the wind,
A wind which had battered its stem,
A wind which had drenched
Both branches and tips
With salt-laden spray.
Windspray which had challenged its growth
As the gales had moulded the shape.
Yet just at the tips
Green heralds of this summer's leaves.
Life through adversity
Hope through strife
I passed a tree this afternoon.

Autumn

Autumn has come to my study.
Three leaves on a tiny beech
Cradled in a plastic pot
Are turning golden copper.
The spindle shoot
Is capped by a bud
Which never burst to leaf.
Will there be spring?

A primula

I saw a primula
This morn
Upon a garden tip
Between stick, stone
And lumps of clay,
Flowering,
It held life's grip.

Oh beauty
Can be strong though frail
Clinging tenacious to life.
Pale pink flower
On dewy leaves
Victor in discard's strife.

The stoat and the rabbit

Hungry stoat
Frightened rabbit
Was there ever
So unequal a fight?

Frozen creature
Darting attacker
Two feeble hops
Rapier thrust to the throat
Soon the contest was done.

Why should
One be so helpless
The other so strong?
Is there a balance in life?
Is what's right in Nature
Wrong in man?
Is justice
Ever settled in strife?

Living near to the clouds

I love to walk
Near the scudding clouds
Along a moorland track
And hear the call
Of a chuckling black grouse
Whirring from threatened attack.

I love to crouch
'Neath grey millstone grit
While wind and rain
Whistle by
And a disturbed ewe
With her two branded lambs
Leaps from her brown bracken lie.

I love to talk
On the close-cropped grass
With a shepherd
Crooked stick in hand
While his two collie dogs
Busying about
Keep the flock as a band.

It's a hard, wild life
Living near to the clouds,
Never far from death or birth.
But it's real and honest
And would that we all
Could live so in touch
With the earth.

A pathway through life

A place for God

'I can't take God's place'
Said Jacob of old
To Rachel of Israel
His wife.
'It's he, not me
That stands in your way'
Of bringing another
To life.

But Rachel's reply
Showed yet other ways
By which to fulfil her plans
When her surrogate slave
Mothered a son.
But was it God's plan
Or man's?

Now millennia on
We've found science's way
To follow the path
Rachel trod.
Yet the question
Unanswered remains,
Have we left any room
For God?

God's in the joy

It seems
We're beginning control
Of each stage from longing
Through conception to birth.
Growth in the womb,
Even nativity's time,
Now all part
Of a day's work done.

Perhaps even soon
We may have the choice
'Tween boy, girl
Single or twin.
So how can we say
Our child is God's gift
When man chooses
Each stage on the way?

Yet!
Who brings the joy
Of a mother and child
Come from no clinic or lab?
And who brings the love
That is every child's due
But on no identity tab?
And who brings the bond
Linking parents and child
And the beauty
Of life that is new?

God's in the joy
As God's in the love
And will be for ever and aye,
Just as God's in the life
Be it humble or great
Rich, poor
Low or high.

She's mine

She's mine
Though I did not,
I could not
Bear her.

She's a part of me,
Part of the love
Joining me with my man,
Part of the love
Making us a family,
She, me and John.

Someday
I'll tell her
Just how she became
Ours.
Then I'll hope
And I'll pray
We'll have shared
Life and love,
She, me and John.
Then we'll really
Be hers
Just as she's mine now.

I took my boy to school

I took my boy
To school this morn
And he just ran away.
I wanted still
To hold his hand
But others claimed his play.

I thought he still
Would cling to me
As only mothers can.
I've had to learn
This schoolday morn
He's begun to be a man.

I thought I had accepted

I thought
I had accepted
That my boy might never walk,
Might never talk,
Might never think,
Like other boys.

But deep down
I hadn't.

I thought
Why should this
Happen to him?
Happen to me?
Happen to anyone at all?

Deep down.
Why us?

I thought
If God is love,
If God is Creator,
Saviour and Maker
Of man,
How can this be?

Deep down
I was torn asunder.

But then I thought
Of Calvary
And how upon its hill
God took to himself
All the cruelty and pain
Of the world he'd made,
All the responsibility
For the evil in his world,
All the pain
In the world of my boy
And his world in me.

So deep down
I began to accept,
Just a little.

First love

I sat down
By a stream
In a wood
One day
Thinking
The end of the world
Had come.

I'd quarrelled
With the very first girlfriend
I'd ever had.
How could one go on?

I sat very still
By the side of that stream,
Digesting
This tragic state,
Till my eye
Caught the sight
Of a big, fat trout
Sliding slowly
Under a rock.

I'll have him,
I thought.
And I did.

Will she pull through?

I feel so helpless.
There's nothing
I can do,
Sitting, watching
My child sleeping,
Wondering
If she will pull through.

Will she really recover?
I ponder,
Clutching at straws of hope.
Even if she gets better
Will she be able to cope?

God,
She's your child
Even more than ours.
You can see the future
Where nothing is
Finally
Beyond your powers.

I've prayed
And I've prayed
For a miracle,
Knowing that it
Just might be.
But what, oh what
If there isn't
And there's no door of hope
For me?

Have I the faith
Have I the trust
To believe that
'Your will be done'?
A young life,
With so much before it,
Suddenly mown down
When it's hardly begun.

We both
Need strength, Lord,
And we both
Are in your plan.
Help her
Help me
For only you can.

My boy's getting married

My boy's getting
Married this weekend
And I've got to be glad
For the lad.
She's a lovely girl
Is his Mary.
I must not be personally sad.

I must not just think
She'll replace me
While I seek
A role that's new.
I must remember
She'll mother his children
And give them the love
That's their due.

If I can think
Of her and her children
Part of our family line,
Then I'll really
Be able to love her
Just as if she were really mine.

Walking the Pentecost way

One night
I gave my life to Jesus,
But next morning
I felt just the same.
While the bishop's hands
Were upon me
I believed
I could live in his name.

I pondered and thought
That next morning
There had to be others like me.
How did they cope?
Who gave them help
To walk their Pentecost way?

I looked at the saints
The world over,
That army of women and men
Who'd lived and died
Struggled and cried
Over ages 'twixt now and then.

I found out
As I studied,
A most surprising line,
For in many ways
Their lives and their actions
Weren't all that different
From mine.

They'd all had
Much the same problems
For all were subject to sin,
Distractions in prayer
And temptations.

So if they had
The same barriers
As seemed to come my way,
Why couldn't I do
As they did
Now I'd given my life away?
Why couldn't I feel
God with me
As I tried to scale the heights
And walk the Pentecost way?

But when I looked
Still closer
I found
They were mainly content
To live
As God had made them,
Doing tasks
For which they were meant.

It was
Because they kept it simple
They were able
To achieve so much.
They held God's vision before them
Safe in the Spirit's touch.

Help me
To keep it simple,
Following day by day,
Not to expect
The spectacular
Walking my Pentecost way.

To a handicapped person

Have you ever thought
How much you have to give?
With all that has been denied you,
You can help others to live.

With so many things
You can't do for yourself
It's easy just to receive.
But there's quite another side to it,
You can help others achieve.

You're still a part of society
Even with what you can't do.
Society needs your handicap
Just to help it win through.

For how without you
Can we see
Life's not just go-getting success?
How can we know
'Neath the surface
The deeper values that bless?

And how, without your example,
Can we meet the challenge
Of care and concern,
As we face up
To all our selfishness
As you help us all to learn?

We have to support each other
Without which we cannot but fall.
You need is our need,
Your strength is our strength,
Your handicap helps us all.

Don't make excuses for God

Don't try
To explain away
Suffering, evil and pain.
Don't make
Excuses for God
When you think
You've been let down
Once again.

Look at the cross
Where you'll see
God shouldering
His world's evil
As he hangs there on a tree.

Calvary's death
Wasn't easy for God
Of that you may be sure,
For as well as the cruelty and pain
He had rejection to endure.

So don't try
To excuse God
For what has happened
To you.
He's entered your world
And stands by your side
Whatever that world may do.

Don't tell me

'Don't tell me'
I used to say,
'To snap out of it,
Buck up
And be cheerful.

'Don't tell me
It's all in the mind.
Smile,
And it will go away.

'Just listen'
I used to ask.
'Listen and let me tell you,
Where I am
And what it feels like.

'How I'm in a tunnel,
Seemingly endless, black,
Where nobody lives,
So I'm not understood
Not even by God.

'Yes, I know there's light'
I used to feel,
'At every tunnel's end.
But in mine
That speck
Never gets any nearer.'

Somehow, where I am
Is always dark, oppressive, dank,
Never different
Whether I went
Forward or back
Or simply stood still.

But then
Someone said to me
Stop
Feeling so guilty,
Being sorry for yourself,
Wanting always your way,
Relying on fixes and pills
While doing nothing
To help yourself.

Start
Accepting whatever life brings,
Valuing and loving yourself,
Sure that others love you
Just as you are,
Knowing you could
And will be well.

Don't tell me
Don't tell me
Don't –
Well, perhaps
Because you're my friend,
I'll try.

Once I loved her

Once I loved her
Now I do not.
Once she loved me
Now she cannot.

Is our love
Like the seasons?
Now autumn is nigh
Will it deepen to winter
When we no longer try?

Can we work
At our marriage
Or is it just leaves
Which are stark?
Can we find buds
For a springtide
In winter's lost dark?

I've never been ill before

I've never been ill before,
Except for a common cold.
I've never had
To take any care,
But now I'm getting old.

It's a nuisance
Not being able
To get about
Doing the things I used.
And it does no good
To my patience at all
So the folk I love
Get abused.

I really don't know
How long I've to lie here.
The doctor refuses
To say,
While my wife
When I ask her
Simply says
I've to keep out of the way.

But thank God
I'm beginning
To get a bit better now
And I'm getting over
The pain.
But am I really thankful
Or shall I soon
Just start over again?

Choose life

I came
Said Jesus
To bring life,
Far more life than before.

And where I am
There is life,
For I am
Way, Truth and Life.

This life
Vital and without end
I offer you.
Choose life,
Choose me.

A staircase to God

One hour nearer God

Whenever
You hear a clock strike,
Think not
That's one hour less,
But rather,
That's one hour
Nearer God.

(After Teresa of Avila)

Can you understand?

Can you understand
How I feel less of a woman
After my surgery?
Part of me has gone,
Gone for ever.
It was the part which gave life,
The part which was a part
Of God's creation.

Oh I know I'm no longer young
But then I'm not old either.
Not old enough to sit aside
And feel that it does not matter
That what made me *me*
Has been cut out
And thrown away
To be burned.

I know it was diseased,
I know it could have killed me,
But it was part of me,
Part of my body, my personality,
My soul, if you like –
And as a person
I'm not just something disposable.

Can you understand?
Can I make you understand?
I don't want reassuring words.
Don't talk to me of
Leah, Ruth and Mary,
Bible women who suffered
Rejection, pain and loss.
Just try to understand
How I feel right now,
Less of a woman.

It can't be true

It can't be true.
It can't, it can't
Be true.

It must be a dream,
A nightmare.
I'll wake up soon
To find it's not true.
No growth, no surgery
No uncertain future.
The doctor's just made
A mistake.

God, you know
All about me.
You know the problems
I face.
And you've got
Your own plans for me.
They simply can't
Include this.

I know I must die
One day
Like everyone else.
But not yet.

It can't, it can't
Be true.

But
If the doctor's right,
He's made no mistake,
What then?

As a Christian
I've said, often enough,
That I'm not afraid
Of death.
At the time
I meant it.
I suppose
Now is the time
I find out.

But I've also said,
God,
That I trust you
With everything
That I have.
Yet when I gave that trust
It did not seem
There was all that much
For you to hold.
I felt in full control.
It's a different matter now,
For my life
Is in your hands.

All of us
Have to trust someone,
Someone who'll
Not let us down.
There's no one I trust
More than you, Lord,
So I trust you
To do your will.
But I ask
As you do it, Lord,
Be close at hand.
The journey's begun,
There's no turning back,
Be it true or not.

It's so hard to be honest

It's so hard to be honest
When honesty gives pain.
It's so hard to be honest
When disappointment
Comes in train.

It's so hard to be honest
When who is bluffing who,
Saying
'How much better you look today;
Knowing it's not true.
And 'Yes, I'm feeling better'
Comes the reply
Which really is a lie.

We know
And she knows
Nothing has really changed.
But we don't want her to know
Nor she, us to know
That nothing is going to change.

We all know,
But nobody knows,
And nobody wants to tell.
Oh how hard it is to be honest.

The will to get well

It's the will
To get well
That's important,
Better than any
Medication you take.
When you say
'I'm going to get better',
That's a sure sign
You're on the make.

Most people aren't hermits

Most people aren't hermits
Alone in their room,
Content with themselves
And God.

Most people need people,
People who speak,
People who touch,
People who listen and care,
And people, too,
Who are just there.

And people who are sick
Really need people,
Not to talk –
They'll do all the talking.
They need to do all the talking
To be in touch
Not with the world outside,
But with themselves within,
To come to terms realistically
With the dull pain which nags
And will not go away.

They need to tell another person,
A real person who will hear.
Not a voice on the phone,
Or a reader of a letter,
Or a sender of cards and flowers.
Just someone who will come
And bring Christ to the room.
Their touch, his touch,
Their care, his care,
Their words, his words,
Just because they are there.

I get so angry

At the height of my pain
I get so angry.
Under my medication
My whole being seems to change.

Then, anyone coming near
Gets my anger
Full force.
Not because of
Who they are,
Why they're here,
What they are to do
Or how it will affect me.

My anger stems
From what is happening
To me –
Which they are escaping.
My life is changing
While theirs flows on still.
My hourglass runs out
While theirs
Seems hardly to have begun.

When the storm's over
I'm so ashamed,
Even though they understand.
I wish in a way
They didn't,
Because that makes me
Feel even worse than before,
And even less able
To copy or repay.

Help me to understand
As I am understood,
And seek to earn the forgiveness,
That forgiveness I'm
So freely given.

Friend or foe?

Friend or foe, Sister Death
How will you come,
When come at the end
You will?

Will your hand
Enfold mine,
Leading over the sill
At the close of a life
That's been full?

Will this body of mine
With its mind and its will
Having given its all,
Lie calmly and tranquilly
Still?

Will I know, Sister Death
Will I hear, your steps
At the door?
Will I know, will I hear
Your voice as you call?

Pray I know, Sister Death
And I'm ready to welcome your call.
For you come as a friend
With a staff not a rod.
Pray I know
That you come from God.

That phone in the night

That phone
That phone
That phone.
Ring, ring, ring in the night.
Steps on the stairs
And a quiet urgent voice
Met with the news
That he'd died.

Silence
And silence,
Just the regular hum
Of the dial-toned receiver
Lowered so slow
From an unwilling ear.

Then darkness
Just light and grey dawn
Of sleepless unbelief.
O God, don't let it
Don't let it
Don't let it be true.

That phone
That phone
I'll never forget
That phone in the night.

'If only'

If only,
Said Martha to Jesus,
You had come at once.
If only,
When our message came,
You had not waited
Two whole days.
You would have seen our brother
While he was still alive.
He would not have died
If you had come,
So said sister Mary too.

If only
I had not been
Out at work,
Missing the bus,
Calling at the shops,
I would have got back sooner,
And sent for the doctor earlier.
I reproach myself,
For if only . . .

If only
The doctor had not been so rushed,
Had come more quickly,
Had spent more time,
Had really seen what was wrong,
Had sent for the ambulance
And rushed him to hospital,
Our dad would not have died.

Your brother will live again,
For life will not end in death.
A promise from Jesus' lips.
'I know' said Martha,
'I know' said I.
As the vicar repeated his words
As we walked into church,
As we stood by the grave,
As he sat by the fire
At the tea when we got back.

If only
I could believe,
Could be really sure
That kind words
Are more than consolation,
That the quality of life
Offered by Jesus
Is more than death,
Is not impaired by its break.

In a sense
Believe it I do,
But in what measure?
Not enough, I know.
Not enough
To do away with the questions,
To eliminate the doubts,
To take away the reproaches.

Convince me, Jesus,
As you did those sisters of old.
Not to bring back our dad,
For I know that cannot be.
But give me the strength
To survive the test
Of life without him and his smile.
Do it for me, or to me, or in me,
Whatever I need that I may believe
And no longer say
'If only'.

Soon it will be time to go

The car's at the door,
The last chrysanthemum wreath
Has shed its yellow petals
Down the path
To join the casque from the chapel of rest.
Soon it will be time to go.

Give me time to be still,
To be calm, to be brave
When I walk down the path
And alone down the aisle
We once walked together,
And stand by the grave,
When it's finally time to go.

When I come back

When I come back
At the end of today,
And live for tomorrow, and on,
Help me to be glad
For the years that have passed
And the life that is promised to be,
When others come back
From me.

Accept you are accepted

Accept
You are accepted
By One far greater
Than you,

Whose name
You neither know nor ask,
Whose will
You seek not now,
Perhaps you may do so later.

Search for nothing,
Perform nothing
Nor intend anything,
Simply accept
You are accepted.

Accepting,
You may not
Be better than you were,
Or believe more than you did,

But in the acceptance moment
Grace conquers sin,
Estrangement departs,
Reconciliation is achieved.

Yet nothing is asked,
Demanded or required.
Simply accept
You are accepted.

Just to say hello

Every day
The postman called.
As 'the house with the post'
We were known.

Yes, I know
Those letters were mainly
For Tom, but somehow
They were also
For me.

It was silly
But somehow it made
Me feel needed.
Just part of things,
You know.

It's all over now.
Only bills seem to come,
For sympathy has long
Died away.

Yes, people are busy
And have lots to do,
Or are perhaps just embarrassed,
Having nothing
To say.

I wish I could hear
Those letters again
As they fall
With a plop on the mat.
Just to say hello.

When others look at me

When others look at me
In a warm and friendly way,
I feel alive,
I feel free.

When others see me
Just the way I am,
I feel accepted,
I feel affirmed.

I need to be accepted,
I need to be affirmed,
Just as a bird needs air
Or a fish the sea,
For acceptance
Is the air of humanity.

Without acceptance
The air becomes thin.
I falter and fail.
Accept me,
Please.

Memory, hold the door

Memory, hold the door,
Keep it aye ajar.
Let not its pictures fade away
Though they come from far.

Memory, keep the voice
Though its owner is still,
Its phrases, tones and accent clear,
Lost beyond death's hill.

Memory, stay the eyes,
Their gaze so steady, true.
Keep the one they guided
Clear before my view.

Memory, memory hold my door,
May it never close.
May your light for ever bind
Me to the one I chose.

Wisdom from of old

I tasted you

You cried aloud,
Piercing my wall of deafness.
Torchlike you shone,
Searching each cranny of blindness.
Fragrance was on your breath
As I too breathed.
So I tasted you,
Yet am still hungry and thirsty
For more.

(After Augustine)

Let your longing be to see God

Let your longing
Be to see God.
Your fear
Be to lose him.
Your sorrow
That you may not cherish him.
Your joy
That he may take you
To himself,
Then perfect peace
Will be yours.

(After Teresa of Avila)

Listen to the lover's call

O you
Who would love,
Seeking fire
Kindle your flame
At my heart.
Looking for water
Draw from the well
Of my eyes.
Harvesting love's thoughts
Glean from my contemplation.

(After Ramon Lull)

Embrace the love of God

Let no one say
I have never known
What to love.

Let him love his brother.
He will love the same love,
For he knows the love
With which he loves,
Better than he knows his brother.

Embrace the love of God,
And by love
Embrace God.

(After Augustine)

Let those rage against you

Let those rage against you
Who have no idea
How hard it is
To discover truth.

Let those rage against you
Who are unaware
How rare it is
To find one in control
Of wandering thoughts.

Let those rage against you
Who have never experienced
The effort acquire
The least speck of knowledge
Of God.

And last,
Let those rage against you
Who have never been caught
In the same trap
In which they find you.

(After Augustine)

A great oneing

And I saw
A great oneing
'Twixt Christ and me.
Was he in pain?
So was I,
And the creatures
That might feel pain
Suffered too.

Yet those
Who knew him not
Suffered pain too.
For all creatures, sun and moon,
Turned their backs.
So all were left in sorrow
Awhile.

So those who loved him
Suffered pain for love.
And those who loved not
Suffered also,
For they failed to comfort
All creatures.

(After Julian of Norwich)

God is all our life

When I saw
The way
God in Trinity
Is,

I saw
Fatherhood, Motherhood, Lordship,
These three
In one God.

In these
Is all our life,
Our being,
Our increasing
And our fulfilling.

(After Julian of Norwich)

The depths of God

Whenever a storm
Blows up
And winds rise high,
Fish dive further
Into the still depths
Of the sea.
Just so,
When all around you
Is sound and fury,
Plunge all the deeper
Into the depths of God.

(After Peter of Alcantara)

The moulding of his fingers

How can you be God
When you've not yet
Been a man?

How can you be perfect
When you've hardly
Been created?

God makes you,
Not you him.
So wait for his hand
To do all
In his time.

Offer him
A pliant heart,
Keeping intact
The being he has given you,
Retaining in yourself
The water from him
The lack of which
Makes you harden,
Resisting the moulding
Of his fingers.

(After Irenaeus)

Child of the Divine Fish

Child of the Divine Fish,★
Take comfort
In the ever-flowing
Streams of Wisdom.
Take the honey-sweet food
Of the Saviour,
Eating with desire,
Clutching in your hands
The Fish.

Fill me
With that Divine Fish,
I pray.

(After a third-century epitaph)

★In the Early Church the fish was a frequent symbol of Jesus.